It was March. Winter was almost over. The buds were opening. The birds were singing in the trees again. The days were getting longer.

A blackbird was looking for things to make the first nest. He found some bark from a silver birch tree. He took it back to the half-made nest.

He was pressing it firmly into the nest, when he saw a mound of dirty wool on the ground. It would be good for lining the nest. He flew down to it.

The blackbird pecked at the dirty wool. It moved. Then it said, "baa … baa … baa." It was a sheep. It was very BIG.

It was a very dirty, thirsty pregnant sheep. "Baa … baa," it said again. The blackbird wanted to help it.

He flew off to find Jelly and Bean. They were by the shed. He chirped at them loudly to go to help the pregnant sheep.

Jelly and Bean rushed to the dirty, thirsty sheep. First, they took her to the water tub, where she had a long drink of fresh water.

Then they took her into the shed, where she lay down on a bed of hay. Then she went to sleep. She did not stir all day.

During the night the sheep gave birth to three little lambs, two girls and a boy! Mother and babies were safe and well.

The next day the blackbird came to visit the sheep and the lambs. Then he chirped the good news to everyone in the farmyard.

"ir"

birds	blackbird
first	birch
firmly	dirty
thirsty	girls
chirped	stir
birth	